A Child's Book of Seasons

SATOMI ICHIKAWA

A Child's Book of Seasons

Heinemann : London

William Heinemann Ltd
10 Upper Grosvenor Street, London W1X 9PA

LONDON   MELBOURNE   TORONTO
JOHANNESBURG   AUCKLAND

First published 1975
Text and Illustrations © Satomi Ichikawa 1975
Reprinted 1982 (twice)
434 94360 6

Reproduction by Colourcraftsmen Ltd.,
Chelmsford, Essex

Printed in Hong Kong by Wing King Tong Printing Co. Ltd.

Inside this book please take a look and see what children do
In snow and sunshine, wind and rain, the changing seasons through.

In the cold and wintry sun
Round the playground children run.

They jump and skip and play at ball
And pushmepullyou by the wall.

Pitter, patter, here's the rain!
The children hurry home again

To stay indoors while long hours pass
And raindrops scurry down the glass.

Here are nurses and soldiers and riders of grace
And elegant ladies in lipstick and lace.

Out comes the sun, and they climb on the sill
To see the bright rainbow bend over the hill.

In spring children play in the garden for hours –
When the sun shines and birds sing it's fun to pick flowers.

Then Mother makes tea for the friends from next door,
With brown bread and honey and lots and lots more.

Leaves rustle softly and whisper and sway:
Can you see in the tree who is hidden away?

Green branches, green birds' nests, green grass or green sea,
There's nothing so green as the world of a tree.

Morning sunlight shimmers in the warm midsummer air:
The countryside is calling for the children to be there.

They pedal down the winding road that leads beyond the town
And stop to see the drowsy cows that browse beneath the sun.

Oooh! how the river tickles your toes
As over the pebbles it swiftly flows

While the little girl beneath the tree
Dreams of a cream and strawberry tea.

Two, four, six, eight,
Trotting through an open gate.

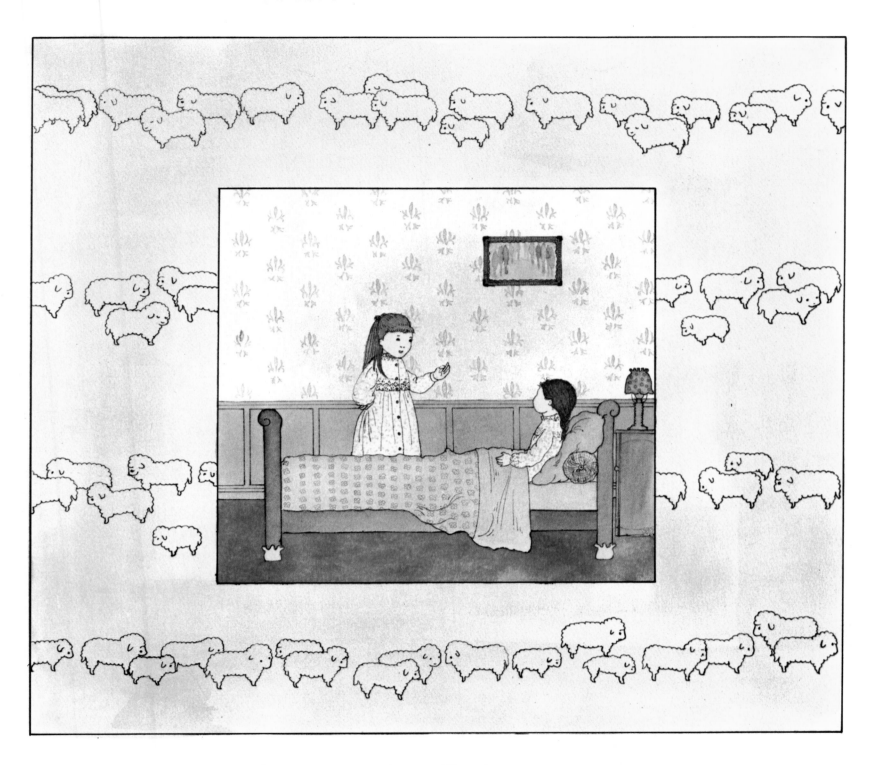

(Try to count those silly sheep
And soon you'll find you're fast asleep.)

In the farmyard the children are scattering feed
For chickens and geese to snatch up what they need.

The mowing of hayfields and clover is done
And the starlings flock in the setting sun.

A long road, a hot sky, the smell of dusty hay –
Summer's nearly over and there's miles to go today.

Carrots, corn and cauliflower are piled up on the cart
But the stubborn little donkey just won't start.

In autumn nuts hang on the tree
Till children come and shake them free.

Leaves turn saffron, russet, brown –
Children catch them sailing down.

Soft in winter falls the snow
Like feathers on the ground below.

Wrapped up warmly children play
With snow and snowmen every day.

In silvery forests the trees are still
As the children trudge homewards beneath the white hill.

Candles and stars give a glimmering light:
Each child hangs a stocking, and whispers 'Goodnight'.